GW00775754

ADVICE
TO THOSE IN
LOVE

The HOLLYWOOD Guide to Romance

Myrna P Barnum*

* friend of the stars

EBURY
PRESS

First published in 2002 by Ebury Press

1 3 5 7 9 10 8 6 4 2

'Myrna P Barnum' is a pseudonym and any similarity between her any living persons is entirely coincidental and no reference to any living person is implied or should be inferred.

Ebury Press
Random House, 20 Vauxhall Bridge Road, London SW1V 2SA

Random House Australia (Pty) Limited
20 Alfred Street, Milsons Point, Sydney, New South Wales 2061, Australia

Random House New Zealand Limited
18 Poland Road, Glenfield, Auckland 10, New Zealand

Random House South Africa (Pty) Limited
Endulini, 5A Jubilee Road, Parktown 2193, South Africa

Random House UK Limited Reg. No. 954009

A CIP catalogue record for this book is available from the British Library

ISBN 0 09 188300 8

All images courtesy of The Kobal Collection

Printed and bound in Hong Kong by Sheck Wah Tong Printing Press Limited

Contents

Welcome

SAD TO BE ALL ALONE IN THE WORLD. Hard to believe it, I know, but I too was once a lonely wallflower locked out of the pleasure garden of love. Yet with application and the odd correspondence course, I managed to escape that old chicken farm in Arkansas and become, even though I say it myself, one of the most sought-after beauties in Hollywood. From there I became a coach without parallel in the on-screen art of amour. Gable, Flynn, Chaplin, oh those terrible boys! There was plenty of experience off-screen too I can tell you. Seven glorious marriages just for starters. But that's another story. The book you hold in your hand is far too small to accommodate me. This book is about you, my little darlings. Follow my lessons carefully and you'll be whisked from the bottom rung of the love ladder to dizzying heights. And, like me, you can stay there too, actively enjoying romance in to your golden years.

Now just where is my darling little Vladimir...

My Golden Rules:

Never be ashamed of your relationship. It's your happiness that counts and to hell with what anybody else thinks

Stan Laurel and Oliver Hardy in *That's My Wife* (1929)

Girls! True love knows no bounds. Trust your primal instincts and pursue the man of your dreams at any cost *

* Think Romeo and Juliet – although this Romeo would have less problem climbing up your balcony than most

Dorothy Lamour and friend in *Her Jungle Love* (1938)

Whirlwind holiday romances rarely work out – particularly with those intense eastern European types *

* My own darling Vladimir is, of course, the rather wonderful exception to this rule

Bela Lugosi and Carol Borland in *Mark Of The Vampire* (1935)

Never date anyone with a drug problem *

* With my first husband, The Kaiser, it started off with slimming pills. I finally lost him in the crowd at Woodstock, never to be seen again

James Stewart in *Harvey* (1951)

Or anyone who drinks
in the morning *

* Well spirits, at least. A glass of wine with your cereal can be rather invigorating

Gene Kelly in *An American In Paris* (1951)

Be patient and persevere. Given time you may grow to love each other's particular idiosyncrasies *

* All but one of my husbands grew to love my collection of celebrity toenail clippings

Madeleine Carroll in *What Money Can Buy* (1929)

Boys! Be realistic, if you're
always expecting Cinderella
to walk into your life, you are
bound for disappointment

Jerry Lewis in *Who's Minding The Store?* (1963)

Tips For Attracting Your Dream Date

Girls! It is my experience, that when the competition from other luscious debutantes gets really tough at the height of the season, a small bribe in a plain envelope can be the difference between eternal happiness and the ugly spectre of lifelong spinsterhood *

* Due to inflation over the decades, I couldn't accurately quote you today's going rate

Clara Bow and Antonio Moreno in *It* (1927)

Let any potential suitor know
that there's a woman under those
rags using every fibre of your
body – dance, gypsy, dance!

Doubling as a finger buffet can
vastly increase your chances
of meeting the right chap.
Particularly the larger sort who
are more than just girl hungry

The Golden Bed (1925)

Boys! While mathematics is not of general importance during courting, a basic understanding of angles can be of some use

Marilyn Monroe and Cary Grant in *Monkey Business* (1952)

When trying to attract a mate,
choose the kind of company who
will show you in your best light

Peter Lupus and Buddy Hackett in *Muscle Beach Party* (1964)

Boyish charm can often bring
results where a more manly
approach has failed

Groucho Marx in *Monkey Business* (1931)

Boys! Never underestimate
good grooming – a genuine
attention to detail in dress can
often have the desired result
with the opposite sex

While you may scoff at poetry in
the company of your peers, in
private the wise bachelor knows
it works magic with the ladies

Bob Hope in *Road To Bali* (1952)

POWER OF
WILL

Men who like their one-night stands should note that small women have the added bonus of being light enough to carry away after you've finished with them

Doris Day and Rock Hudson in *Pillow Talk* (1959)

Are You Right For Each Other?

If you want to know how he'll treat you in 20 years time, observe his relationship with his mother

Patricia Hitchcock and Robert Walker in *Strangers On A Train* (1951)

If you can't decide which one is
the man for you, why not store
test them in a direct comparison?

Cary Grant, Katharine Hepburn and James Stewart in
The Philadelphia Story (1940)

Men! Beware of gold-diggers.
Who are you kidding? Nobody
is that interesting, not even you

Marilyn Monroe, Lauren Bacall and Betty Grable in
How To Marry A Millionaire (1953)

Beware of those high-
maintenance types, your
toiletries bill alone could bankrupt
you and you might never get
the chance to use your own
bathroom again

Frank Sinatra and Gina Lollobrigida in *Never So Few* (1959)

Those crazy minxes who keep
your friends laughing all weekend
rarely turn out to be the
companion you'd care to spend
the rest of your life with

Arthur Freed and Herb Brown in *Hollywood Revue* (1928)

Avoid jealous types

Doris Day and Allyn McLerie in *Calamity Jane* (1953)

Girls! Try not to fall for
first date show-offs

Cary Grant and Irene Dunne in *The Awful Truth* (1937)

Wear something to please your date. A big-dame hunter, for instance, will always enjoy bagging a cat with spots

Clark Gable and Jean Harlow in *Red Dust* (1932)

If you are nervous about a date, don't try too hard; wear something simple that you feel comfortable in

Marlene Dietrich in *Kismet* (1944)

Boys! You might have first date nerves too, but keep a steady hand in order to avoid those unsightly shaving cuts

Humphrey Bogart and Lauren Bacall in *Dark Passage* (1947)

On a first date, keep conversational enquiries on a polite, impersonal level

Jeanette MacDonald and Maurice Chevalier in *Love Me Tonight* (1932)

Writing and performing a
concept album about your
new partner on the first date
can appear a little too keen

Peter Sellers amd Claudine Longet in *The Party* (1968)

Strangely, dial-out pizza is not
every girl's idea of a
romantic meal for two

Cary Grant and Rosalind Russell in *His Girl Friday* (1940)

In these litigious times, those with a history of accidents involving candles and cigarettes should always use the fire-resistant metal sleeves provided by many top-class restaurants

Sylvia Sydney and George Raft in *Mr Ace* (1946)

Always refrain from baby talk in public as it can offend those of a delicate constitution

Robert Walker, Rags Ragland and Hedy Lamarr
in *Her Highness And The Bellboy* (1945)

Choose a venue that will show you in your best light. If you can't 'go-go', the local dance club is a strict no-no! This counts double if neither of you is strictly a mover

Helen Twelvetrees in *The Cat Creeps* (1930)

Maintaining eye-contact at
all times is of utmost
importance on a first date

Kirk Douglas, Barry Sullivan, Lana Turner and Gilbert Roland in
The Bad And The Beautiful (1952)

If a young lady should decline
your request for the next dance,
a gentleman should always accept
the refusal with good grace

James Stewart and Marlene Dietrich in *Destry Rides Again* (1939)

While drink can help you relax on a date, an excess may make you less suitable company

Cliff Edwards, Joan Peters and Buster Keaton in *Parlour, Bedroom & Bath* (1931)

I'm ashamed to say it's true.
Chocolate will get you everywhere

Elaine Devry and Walter Matthau in
A Guide For The Married Man (1967)

Always give careful consideration to ambience when choosing the venue for that all-important first kiss

Charles Boyer and Jean Arthur in *History Is Made At Night* (1937)

Be prepared for unwanted reactions from your best friends when you finally introduce them to your new partner. Remember they do not share the benefits of your love blinkers

Spencer Tracy and Roscoe Karns in *Woman Of The Year* (1942)

When a young gentleman offers
to entertain you at the piano
make sure he keeps both hands
on the keyboard

Cary Grant and Mae West in *I'm No Angel* (1933)

Try not to fall asleep when
he talks about his job

Gilbert Roland and Norma Talmadge in *Camille* (1927)

If it turns out her family belong
to a minority religious sect, it's
probably best to try and play
along until she's legally yours

Maria Minzenti and Walther Carl Meyer in
Der Siebente Jungle (1925)

Particularly clever pets can
be used to show pushy or
boring dates to the door

Irene Dunne and Cary Grant in *The Awful Truth* (1937)

If you're going to stay over
at his place make sure his
mother doesn't mind

Anthony Perkins and Janet Leigh in *Psycho* (1960)

Boys! Having been a bachelor for so many years, you may need to brush up on some of your social skills. Table manners, for instance

Jack Lemmon in *The Apartment* (1960)

Keep your abode in tip-top order. The state of a single man's bathroom can be the last straw when a woman comes to make her crucial decision about you

Cyd Charisse and Robert Taylor in *Party Girl* (1958)

When a girl says she loves fur she means a mink from Macy's, you klutz! Body hair should be kept in good order if you don't want to remain single forever *

* With the right open-minded gentleman, waxing can actually make for interesting foreplay

Michael Landon and Yvonne Lime in
I Was A Teenage Werewolf (1957)

Girls! While a large stone for a Valentine's present seems to show a lack of imagination on the part of a suitor, try not to appear downhearted. With a woman's magic the lesser male can still be shaped into the man of your dreams.

Freshman Love (1931)

While a man's generosity will go a long way, it can rarely compensate for basic errors regarding personal grooming

Lupita Tovar in *The Cat Creeps* (1930)

Keep him in check by showing him who's boss at an early stage *

* That reminds me of an interesting month I spent in the Swiss Alps with my Aikido instructor Johann

Honor Blackman and Sean Connery in *Goldfinger* (1964)

Girls, a quick tip from someone who knows! Many of our older bachelor friends suffer from Sweaty Neck Syndrome. It is always wise to carry a handy towel for more intimate amorous embraces

William Powell and Hedy Lamarr in *The Heavenly Body* (1943)

Desperately Seeking Anyone

However desperate you might become, copping a feel on the bus is a totally unacceptable form of courtship *

* The fact that I met, as you may remember from my memoirs, the vile Count Oloroso this way, simply serves to underline my point

Patsy Kelly and Stuart Erwin in *The Party's Over* (1934)

STRIKE

HANS

Your search for a suitable partner
might seem hopeless, but
resorting to cruising the graveyard
for a date is sadly deemed
unacceptable by society

Vague allusions to an imaginary inheritance can certainly buy you the female attention you crave...

Mae Busch, Stan Laurel and Dorothy Christie in *Sons Of The Desert* (1933)

But remember: those white lies
can put you in an awkward
position further down the line,
especially if you reveal your true
hand directly after your belle
has given you her all

Sharon Lynne and Stan Laurel in *Way Out West* (1936)

Girls! Never date beneath yourself,
even when you're really stuck.
Those grateful types can be
hard to shake off

Miriam Hopkins and Fredric March in
Dr Jekyll and Mr Hyde (1931)

It is an offence in many countries to date men against their will by use of force. Though a prison term might help you to confront that latent chick thing you've always suppressed

Virginia Huston in *Woman From Headquarters* (1950)

Be prepared for those tricky
in-laws not taking your
proposal seriously

Dorothy Lamour, Bob Hope and Anthony Quinn in
Road To Morocco (1942)

If you really love her,
you'll let her have the wedding
ceremony she truly wants

Edgar Barrier and Acquinetta in
Tarzan & The Leopard Woman (1946)

Rather than following tradition,
many modern couples prefer to
make a more personal statement
to seal their vows

Lon Chaney in *Where East Is East* (1929)

The security that marriage affords can make it a good time to tell clingy best friends what you really think of them

Lorraine Howard and Florence Newton in *Wedding Bells* (1924)

I know it goes against all the rules, but if you don't want to lose her, I'd wait until she's legally yours before you tell her about your love of dressing up *

* My second husband Lord Barnabas ruined too many of my Chanel suits for me to ever totally forgive him

Buster Keaton in *Parlour, Bedroom and Bath* (1931)

Choose the moment carefully to
tell him that family tradition
insists that your grandmother
should witness consummation

Here, Prince (1932)

In The Bedroom

Better to make sure that you share
the same interests in the bedroom
before it's too late

Joan Crawford and Fred Mac Murray in *Above Suspicion* (1943)

If you're involved in an gay
S&M affair it is probably better
to confess all before it becomes
a problem. Any bright pin of a
wife is bound to catch on
sooner or later

Boys! While it can be a pleasing experience for a lady, the street is never the place to look for her G-spot; this is especially true for those not entirely sure where it is

While an erectile enlargement pump can be cumbersome and embarrassing to mention, tests have proved it to have the desired effect...

John Barrymore in *Romance In The Dark* (1938)

Although in extreme cases results
can never be guaranteed

Cleopatra (1925)

All couples should bear in mind where the primitive tangle of the marital hearth ultimately leads *

* Though with the right team of nannies you can go for decades without encountering the little cherubs

Baby LeRoy and W. C. Fields in *It's A Gift* (1934)

As time goes by, wrinkles are an inevitability. But any talk of plastic surgery for an older partner should be broached with the utmost care and tact *

* See the index for my personal recommendations

Frank Orth and Ann Codee in *Sleepy Head* (1931)

Try to keep those rituals of daily hygiene out of sight so that your partner can continue unhindered to worship you as a deity *

* None of my husbands were ever allowed to see me on the toilet or without make-up

Mae West and W. C. Fields in *My Little Chickadee* (1940)

When men lose interest in the bedroom side of things, they will try the most ridiculous of excuses, but there is only so many times a full-blooded woman can stand for the "I thought I heard a cobbler in the hall" line

William Gargan and Vivienne Osbourne in *She Asked For It* (1937)

If all the parties are consenting,
wife swapping can be a lovely way
to liven up a dull winter's evening

The Fight (1931)

However good you think you are
at it, amateur glove-puppetry
alone has rarely saved a troubled
relationship from doom

Paul Muni and Ann Dvorak in *Scarface* (1932)

If all else fails, the internet can offer the option of the mail-order bride. Everything you ever dreamed of easily assembled in an afternoon

Elsa Lanchester and Boris Karloff in *Bride of Frankenstein* (1935)

There are, of course, alternatives
to the love between a man and
a woman, but due to the lack of
space, they are not dealt
with in this book

Jack Lemmon and Tony Curtis in *Some Like It Hot* (1959)